BROKEN
THINGS

Olúwapèlúmi F. Sàlàkó

BROKEN THINGS

(poetry)

Olúwapèlúmi F. Sàlàkó

Copyright ©2018 Olúwapèlúmi Francis Sàlàkó

ISBN: 978-978-964-186-4

All rights reserved.
No part of this book may be reproduced, distributed, stored in a retrieval system or transmitted, in any form or by any means, electronic, electrostatic, magnetic tape, mechanical, photocopying, recording or otherwise without prior written permission from the Publisher.
For information about permission to reproduce selections from this book, write to info@wrr.ng
National Library of Nigeria Cataloguing-in-Publication Data

Printed and Published in Nigeria by:
Words Rhymes & Rhythm Limited
Suite C309, Global Plaza Plot 366, Obafemi Awolowo Way, Jabi District, Abuja, Nigeria.
08169027757, 08060109295
www.wrr.ng

DEDICATION

For
    my   mother,   *Segilola*
    whom I carry within me

ACKNOWLEDGEMENT

Acknowledgement is due to the editors of the following journals — Prachya, Tuck, Dwarts, Gifted hands anthology— which some of the poems in this chapbook have previously featured wholly, partly or with other titles.

CONTENTS

Dedication 5
Acknowledgement 6
Contents 7
the arsonist's views..................................9
Of boys who has seen god 10
A large empathy.....................................11
Another black boy..................................13
Lost boys..14
Heart cantos 16
To love a woman....................................18
When we talk about old lovers..............19
Transfiguration.......................................21
About girls who are butterflies 22
a confession..24
of catacombs and chastity 26
Crank shrapnels......................................27
Our children to war - Yemeni Minister................28
Tales we only tell in our head 31
Satin 33
Broken things...34
Men who will never return home..........36
What my society calls abstract..............38
Vertical joints...40
A lost poem 42

A poem for a dead lover 43
of totem and gods 45
Beautiful Nubia: acrostic 46
Ajilete 48
Fela Kuti : epiphany in lieu of an elegy 49
The poet reminisces a jaunt 50
A cursive place 53
For Alice and everyone that has gone ahead 55
songs I sang of my mother 56
Ilorin 58
Egungun 60
Arundhati Roy 61
SUMMARY 63

Broken Things

THE ARSONIST'S VIEWS

Olúwapèlúmi F. Sàlàkó

OF BOYS WHO HAS SEEN GOD

the church is not the only place to find the lord.
sometimes a woman's body is enough. you find
sacredness in brothels down the street
or at the right turn, before reaching the mosque.

there, boys, young boys like us behold the face
of god: pink. hold hands with him
and walk through narrow spaces and damp earth
where electricity cackles loosely – call this land holy

this is a form of worship too.

tomorrow, if you see men talking to a crowd
about how the face of god is calm, or Morose or harsh,
don't call them heresy.

A LARGE EMPATHY

I
On nights like this when boys like me
get enveloped in fear and longing
and loneliness. when I seek for words to
fill the hole tide has etched in my body.

Nights like this when I become longing hands
in search of whom to hold, shoulders
to rest on.

II
life is a mirage, your bird leaves you
for greener branches. times cast your palms
outside in the cold, causing it to whither. and
some latest news cast your body into war.
leaving you a ruined city of carcasses and
ashes & smokes. sons straggling around to
glue the ruins of their mother's gourds and
elders filling the bullet holes on their

walls with
water.

III
I don't want young boys like me to walk around
with songs of sadness in their mouth, I don't want
boys walking with their mind bare and their tongue
tangled in their mouth. I don't want boys to quiver
silently because of the fear of mockeries. i don't want
boys with unpleasant memories stuffed in their throats.

ANOTHER BLACK BOY

for Ope Adetayo, a fellow wayfarer

You know how empty it is
to walk alone on long solitary roads.
how your heart sizzles when you
see paintings of familiar evil
and kindred hammocks. how
your mouth twitches when you
want to break into a run, but falls
endlessly into a pool of tear

walk into your stackings
when you need to breathe.
therein sits a bird, a
black spirit – your spirit.

speak your stale portmanteau
and wear your face to a laugh.
you are another black boy headed
for the mars.

Olúwapèlúmi F. Sàlàkó

LOST BOYS

for boys like us
who can't find
the path home.

for boys like us
who can't recognize
the sound of home bell

for boys whose
palms have no lines.
boys with bare chests.
and little feet:

- never lose sight of yourself.
  wear your country on your skin.
  like your father's old coat

- search within yourself when you need light.
    there's a fire within you that crackles in the dark

- you are not alone in your struggles.
    I am your brother in arms.

- give yourself to the air
    & watch your body levitate

Broken Things

- be your pill and your succor
  there's a miracle beneath your skin

- you can never be lost
   home is there in your heart

for boys like us hiding in my throat.

Olúwapèlúmi F. Sàlàkó

HEART CANTOS

We were kids
when we first held hands and

ignited fire in our bellies.
  - that evening we floated

on seas of promises unsaid and
marked a sheet of the book

that now houses our graph.
Every night brings home reminisces

of our rendezvous with its closure.
it is amazing how love can be fire and

Sea at equal portions without one eating
the other. how your smile still serenades my

heart like a nightingale rendition/ bestrode
me like a colossus. my belly still dissolves into

fireflies and butterflies on a *moonbow* night

and my face bones into an unplaced tapestry.

will you take me by hands and walk me leisurely
again while the sun eases into the night's pocket?

TO LOVE A WOMAN

a woman's body is filled
with different musical notes,
So many bordereau. songs
to play by the pianos.
you never know which song
you play that suits and
you never know the ones that
will leave them on the balustrade
weeping for days. every part hurts
& you don't know how to ease them.
sometimes I am tempted to ask a woman;
how do you like me to love you?

some women love to be explored and thrust,
some cry at the sight of your shaft, they say
it's demeaning. so they fly about howling the songs
of trauma. others want you to play them a treble clef,
they want high notates. I have encountered some who
want to be treated like my father's hoary portmanteau.
some want to be treated like birds

WHEN WE TALK ABOUT OLD LOVERS

    for Timamee

where are you now? who now lies beside you?
last night was a tough one, they say it's hard
to ward off the voices of your old lovers from
your skin. they come to you in a hard fashion,
hitting hard against the walls of your heart

they say the smell of your old lovers
are forever glued to you. they never really vanquish. you catch
a whiff of their scent every now and then. from
the terraces of your rear, to the alley that
leads to your bosom. not even sandpaper
will clear off the marks they left on you.

our hearts are fragile, lucid and weak. they

let us down too many times where they ought to
toughen. they weaken as the wave of time slaps back
those memories at their doorposts.

don't be broken, my mother's body is full of stories too.
tales told only by her eyes and her empty sighs, stories
beholden by the marks left by my father's snipe

Wear your feet to a dance, she will make some fire
tonight. the soil will have some merry. a woman
dies only when her soul is dead.

TRANSFIGURATION

It is unclear why memories are backlogs
   Of heinous things, stacks of dark and
Purple things hanging on the necks of
   The pearly gate turning lush green things
Into brown. Death has no formal dress
   Except the amoebic gowns we know it
To wear. Plain and simple things
   Today, backlash of a motorcade tomorrow
Showering you with rains like the Holy Ghost.
   This was how my grandmother's soul
Sipped away in bed while my mother was
   On watch. Slippery things dribbling through
The bone marrows and strands of tiny
   Voices bypassing your eardrums. Like
The sky is too quiet but the cloud is a
   Loud neighbor trying to drench me in its
Arm (but I'm not wet yet)

ABOUT GIRLS WHO ARE BUTTERFLIES

for Gobir.

Girls like you have learnt the art of living.
you fold your worries and fears and tears
into a mould of gourd and you head to the
river with it with a smile sketched in your
face.

your mouth is a country of words. every
meeting with you rails me to different
cities. you speak like a mixture of wine
and nitrous oxide. you amble me into awe
as laughter and cackles fall from your mouth.
sometimes I wonder if your lips have a hole.

learn to wash away the stains from yesterday
and burn your fears into powder and color your

feet with its ashes. on your face is a map of the
path that leads you home, you will never stutter
for light shall guide you home.

A CONFESSION

It is true how I can be an umbra
and a lost language on the lips
of stolen boys. How I can be
be a deserted home on a Tenerife sea
and a broken minute-hand on the
chest of a wall clock. how sometimes
i am a tourist in my own body. and
i amble in boulevards of gauntness.
how i resemble
too much the news coming from my
mother's old
radio:

"two boys took their troubles
to drown in a river nearby but
she sipped them instead"

how distrust found its root in my
boulevard
and windows no longer usher light and
birds no longer wear the definition of
freedom.
& water & land do not offer safety

how most times I am afraid of growing
old
to become like him – my father. i don't

want
to be a failed dream. how he had wanted
to play football but ended up in the middle
of a fat fog. I found a picture of
him where his smile looked like mine
last night in the belly of a fading
leather box and my bowel grunted.

I swear, I won't lie that I don't breach myself
or drink from my own sea. say pleasure/gold/
worship/honor/death/destruction/god.
but I don't
want to eat, walk, pray, Run, read, sleep, because
the preacher says.

I keep waking and running & evolving
because I am a god in the image of god.

and I don't want to falter so I break and
Mend again because only the broken survive.

Olúwapèlúmi F. Sàlàkó

OF CATACOMBS AND CHASTITY

CRANK SHRAPNELS

I found this song in the middle of
dark places and piercing catchwords,
formaldehyde air and an unplaced
Requiem
that wears a rhythm that resemble me
 so much –

This song was sung in a distant place
where gloom was chiefly in a
communal fest
and it feels just like here – home

How starkness is a flower that blooms
in
every sphere of the world and how
children never
become free of their childhood
memories and never
mend from the little broken things
they condescend into
as they blossom into adulthood to
become sad poets,
and suicide bombers /militants /killers.

The new telegraph reeled out this
morning;

Olúwapèlúmi F. Sàlàkó

"let us close schools and send
our children to war - Yemeni minister

Picture young boys lying inhumed
in the earth. and dreams lying in
craters
– unclaimed, unlived, dead – just like
their
owners. Or youths carving their
mouths into
a request to kids from Maryland to fill
a
bank teller. Or grieving mothers
searching for
the carcasses of their sons.

I found this poem waiting to be
hanged on a guava tree.
An ember war

The last time I saw her
She was in that red kimono
-vestige

Her head buried in the
grey balaclava like a cumulus Cloud
herself retroflexing a Fez.

Staffed loofah and daffodils ,

Broken Things

She bore a collanded palette
an artist's cry.

a perforated Fleur-de-lis and
a caricature of everything rotten
and burnt

pestled things in a contracted
boloche -withered rosemary
and damp upholsteries.

Leaving home for pastures
Incognito and rainbow of feelings
Chiefly.

I imagine her again whistle
and walk past the church after
the turning –

On a December evening.
Memory overlapping into a sweeping
wind
and her face a castrated history
                              -
indiscernible/undetermined/hazy/forgo
tten/lost

she pawned a furtive ambivalence
shared in between an undetermined
War

Olúwapèlúmi F. Sàlàkó

A revolt// choice// little things //
abyssal

I don't know if she has found peace
Or certitude or other things she sought
But women like her subsist in swamps
and can be found scarcely – darkly defiant.

TALES WE ONLY TELL IN OUR HEAD

In wars,
we never find the
missing body parts.
we only count the
stars on the bodies
of the dead. and perform
ablution with their bloods
        -sulphur-
and pick the remains of
our father's broken
gourds.

voices around fire resonate
in anguish and pain. our wind
pipes get stuffed with cries of
eli eli lama saba thani

we let their half-burnt body
    or drilled body
        or smashed heads
  form a shape
on our minds.

then we paint a street
on our memory lanes.
        then we stretch a corner
and there we dump their images
and struggles and dreams.

and sometimes we visit them there.

SATIN

this is how beings melt under
half-lit candles. In rooms that
hold smell of ashes from cigar.
how water from beings forms a
unison of soul. waters falling
into themselves to purify
blackened souls. two lakes
coming together to form a sea.

a cleric says men who
sniff themselves will be fed to fire.
when does love become rewritten
from the back to sound like evil?

my heart is a leaf falling from the
arms of a tree. I keep falling
                and falling
                          falling.
into my own thoughts – sympathy
for humanity. I shudder and cower.
I hide in the unlit part of my belly.
there I become wishing letters
till we won't have to hide ourselves
when we crawl into each other.

Olúwapèlúmi F. Sàlàkó

BROKEN THINGS

I know these songs of grief,
I once lived in its cracked walls
I have threaded the paths of pain
and loss too – grounded and battered.
the tongue of sadness is a baked
cow's tail – burnt and black.
a mad dog running across a silent street,
her tail on her head.
tears sometimes are white milk trickling
down my grandmother's fallen breasts
– shrunken and dry and barren
Mother is a water of different bodies of rivers,
sometimes I am lost on the way home
is there such a map that leads one to solitude ?
every soul is free to grow and live and find its way
– to peace and love and salvation.
joy is a city within the confines of sadness,
first to dig and swim and struggle and be free
the water of happiness tastes sweet to
a victor's heart

of what importance is light when there is no darkness?
to fight is to cry and be sad. to grieve and lack
and be bent by the wind of time. to win is to sing the
songs of defeat accompanied by a long line of owl
and still be whole. to live is to understand that life is a
continuous contest, it shall take your voice and
give you an ink of water to write with. yesterday,
my dead grandmother's soul came visiting,
she smelt of flowers forming a Bond,
she sang of a wonderful end to a strong soul

Olúwapèlúmi F. Sàlàkó

MEN WHO WILL NEVER RETURN HOME

my country is no safe haven,
all the roads here have death enshrined
in their bodies. a man will leave home
to plant his own sweat
but will not live to see the
sun rise in the sky.

his splintered head and bloodied
mouth will usher light into the
day. his bag and phone lie apart
like a distressed mother's chest.
his brain matter bring borno very close.
the smell of fresh blood and flailing pulse
paint the fickleness of life, right in my sight.

a rumpled man in the crowd will belch and say:
we don't know the sins his mother has committed.
and an old woman will sigh and tilt her head sideways.

Broken Things

his ID card says he is a pastor.

Olúwapèlúmi F. Sàlàkó

WHAT MY SOCIETY CALLS ABSTRACT

I don't know how a fellow man
will say to another man

    You will burn in hell

because you choose to love
and keep god's command

how does one say die and burn defiantly
with hatred clutched in their teeth?

how do you watch another man
roast and die a hot death.

i have read and heard of men
who died watery death in distant places because
they say death is cheap in a foreign land. what
do we say of a chicken death, right in your own land?

How do you name men who kill their
brothers because of varied conceptions?

does the man who let fire lick his brother not *shaytan*?

Olúwapèlúmi F. Sàlàkó

VERTICAL JOINTS

let us pretend
>that this man
tasted his own
blood and called it
water. and that
his own mother
tasted her water
and named it fire.

and S/he believed
>that the west
exists to plump
your illusion and
to fuel your dispatch
to a tenerife of odium.

there's a disease
>inside you that
must be hurt
and burnt if you
must live and
survive wholly.

peep into your
>chest pocket,
there's a new life
beneath old lives.

Broken Things

like train stations
under cities.

Olúwapèlúmi F. Sàlàkó

A LOST POEM

The stars are full of dreams
of dead men, each waiting to be
Harvested. There is something
always missing in the world,
from a misplaced fuse in a circuit,
undersupplied nutrient to a flower,
my missing face in the family picture
and like the girl – my mother
searching for a
man she loved in my head. Sometimes
She examines my face or ear or
Call me out to feel the tempo of
Him in my response – perhaps it is
Laced with spikes of vodka or
It has girls on skimpy skirts
And drowny eyes in them.
I don't know why I feel lost every time
I try to capture my story in words,
why
The right spellings evade me and
Dark things invade my memory
And why the bottle cannot contain me
The last time I tried

A POEM FOR A DEAD LOVER

Your favorite gown still sits elegantly
In my room like an antique – a coveted
National heritage. Your smell still litters
In my veins and I now smell faint things.
Deep in my heart, there is a part burning
And burning still but not dying. Your memories
Lighten and darken me at the same time. I
Don't understand how things could be torn and new.
I find your face in every passing girl, but all wear
Faint, disheveled and unclear forms. Maybe this
Is how dying men feel. Your picture still lives in
My jean pocket and I try to trade your memories
With fire and wind but it all rushed back to me
In one gusto. My eyes are taut now, they have drowned
So many times in the sea of their own

water.
there is no gauge for pain and my
pains no longer leak
With cigarette smokes

OF TOTEM AND GODS

Olúwapèlúmi F. Sàlàkó

BEAUTIFUL NUBIA: ACROSTIC

It started like this in 2000:
I stopped myself from wandering
Inside stalagmites and rummaging caves.
Since the first time in my Father's redolent room
at Ibadan. The empty spaces in the little boy
I was filled up with drops of things - Things I
Call tranquil and healing. How can a stranger
Invade your body and call it home?

A prophet who lives in a house by the sea:
Martha's grey//now
Sitting//all alone//in her little house//by the sea
And every moment//passing//brings her closer//still
To the one//she loves//the most
Martha's gone//now

You will know you've found an
Old textbook when you find a bonfire
On its skin.

Here comes the
Great sage in a coat of wind
and a voice that carry birds
In it – feverish like an ejaculation

The gods must have filled his mouth
With water and fire and too much wisdom.

AJILETE

Roads here are like water pipes
leading you definitely into your parlor/
Bedroom/toilet. the roads mask a
German garment aloof a low budget.
Everyman wears a manic on their
Face – they say it is an aftermath
Of a harsh economy.

At night, the districts here dissolve
into an open necropolis. One parting the
Other like the face of the man who first
Came to this town, Ogunlola.

You will not be greeted by an empty air
here, with the help of a nearby church or
Mosque or pub.

I don't sleep at night lately,
Some wild voices roar near my windowsill
sending rocky shrapnel – like Taraa
at my memory of a calm, morose home.

Broken Things

Olúwapèlúmi F. Sàlàkó

FELA KUTI : EPIPHANY IN LIEU OF AN ELEGY

Black, defiant and venomous like his yabbis,
He must have devoured a genie's head or whole.

Warring sorrow, tear and blood and guns and bone
Into wrestle. Kinned with Marley, toyitoyi, Amandla awethu -

Masked with ashen, the remnant//aftermath of a rebellious
Fire. Cheek full of breeze and thunderstorm and everything

Poisonous to Abacha//idi-agbon.
Merging struggle
and passion into Voices. You will look for him

on earth and find smokes clustered in the middle of a
Serious thing. Immortal like his name, Kuti.

THE POET REMINISCES A JAUNT

Lafiaji. a jaundice slanted fateful travel.
drivers here will get you sandwiched,
In between human and anthropoids alike.
smell rouses and collides at the ledge
of the atmospheric arm - foul and treacly.

the road here has many tears to its
body. tattered and upsetting. motor
falls in and out of its mouth every now
and then. the metal frame rumbling against
my creaking bod – heads collide to an uproar.

Fulani women are such spectacle to lay
eyes on from afar. tall, tatted bonnie char.
a nigh gaze will squirt a taste of carbide
in your mouth.

The market here will bring embalmed souls

alive. grain, corn, rice, beans sit in iron
fellowship. Rams and meat set in rows, there
owners search for buyer in your eyes.

Gbugbu. here eventide shares paternity with
day light. almajirs cramm the rocky spaces
like soldier ants after a rendezvous –
gangly
abject boys. a bestial competition with
the Nupe natives. every boy here rides a bike.

Sabo will serve you an unleavened bread
garnished with mad folks to go with. young
Hausa boys will run their bikes into you.
-echoes of Allah Akbar will soon rent the air to
ransom.

A mad Fula wields his rod fiercely at the teeming
flies like a herd of cows. he pops his eyeballs to their limit

as he treats himself to a cane of sugar
at its stretch.

Head droops like the phallus.

Home is nowhere to be found here.
even the rooms
form a gang against the air. heat
forces you to a
tortuous sleep.

I clutch tightly to my crisp wallet. It
holds memories.
-neatly tucked modules, a memorabilia
of sort.

Olúwapèlúmi F. Sàlàkó

A CURSIVE PLACE

I am afraid of dreaming about water and darkness.
Water has a way of lounging me to endlessness,

darkness aids it to plug you further into nothingness
It speaks a slippery language that I don't know,

I don't want to fall and lose my soul.
like I am falling into a hollow well without rings

or rubicle to hold on to. and falling into nought,
still. The first time I dreamt of the sea,

it had a late sun slipping into its chest.

When I told my mother about it, she stood

by the unhinged entrance in a foreign smile.
says that I am the frightened captain

of a sinking

canoe or a lighthouse without fire
  -but I am here again

whatever ends a bad dream is a rumpled bed
or fallen pillows and sweaty forehead and

sometimes a panting chest. heaving
Fear and anxiety.
then sometimes these memories will return to you in the day

taunting and pranking you to a fretful withdraw
a rejuvenation of smelling seaful cartographies.

FOR ALICE AND EVERYONE THAT HAS GONE AHEAD.

Every night I go to sleep with your
Memories playing wildly in my veins
And engulfed by the empty spaces in history
Filled with sadness momentarily.

I carry your bodies and wrap them in
Small modules – i save them in the secret
Places of my body. Then I carry your
Memories in my chest like a totem.

I can't remember the other names vividly
Like my grandmothers. But your faces
Still tango in my head. You are broken
Mirrors – unclaimed dreams, broken promises
and forgotten things

I don't cry in this poem because broken
Things can become beautiful. broken mirrors
Can retroflex. But don't become shards and

Hurt our feet.

Olúwapèlúmi F. Sàlàkó

SONGS I SANG OF MY MOTHER

My mother is an artist of light
and a sailor pacifying the sea to

Peace. because we are born to rage
and pain; mother offers light, warmth

and shelter to statuettes. She plays songs
Sang in the tongue of her mother and the

Mothers who hath in the long lineage of her
own Mothers as she balms caterpillars to
Butterflies.

A metal thing fell from the zinc roof
Of the adjacent quarters
In the compound

and its thud reverberated many times in my
chest:

Maami, Maami
will you leave without me?

Not all fallen things are broken. And not all broken
Things are fallen. Fire had to lick gold so many
times to glitter.

ILORIN

I watched from my hostel
Apartment how this town has
So many faces
Beneath a purdah like
a recursive history and how the boxes
With yellow color
On their skins cram
nearly the same space
Simultaneously leaving no space for
the pedestrian on
The university road.

I arrived here feeling unanimous and
Undecided like the night I had my first
Kiss. I still fluff and break into laughter
From the smell of a funny pronunciation
From an innocent korope driver or an
Unsuspecting indigene.

Do not look a woman in the eye
Or recall the remaining elements
Of the legendary generalissimo, Afonja's
Battles.

Broken Things

Little things will stick around you
like your first lessons at the preschool
But you will be safe.

Olúwapèlúmi F. Sàlàkó

EGUNGUN

Reverberated voices of the
ancestors. The masker wears
the shadow of the gods like his skin
(invisible//sacrosanct//Untouched)
armed with pankere to
Ward off Ibi

Ayangalu who leads this procession
with the chanters comes first.
then the Atokun who guides the
Masquerade by hand follows.

When you get to the road,
Pray that The journey is not
long and dusty, for Awodagbese's
Garb tags fortuity.

Iba! Ara orun, the bridger of space
The messenger of time, the harbinger
Of news.

ARUNDHATI ROY

The fighter woman bending freedom
Into expression. She sketches all the

tiny dots between activism and arts
And wears her own voice top-over into

Demiurge. Strung together in ideas like
Twilight. From the hill station of Shillong

To ooty and Kerala. The revolutionary
Thing fighting wind…

OLÚWAPÈLÚMI FRANCIS SÀLÀKÓ, poet and essayist, is a sophomore student of History and International Studies at the University of Ilorin. His poems have recently appeared or are forthcoming in Tuck magazine, Dwarts, Prachya Review, WS Africa, elsewhere. His essays appear in medium. Sàlàkó is a commonwealth youth correspondent and curator of Wakaabout, a street photography project dedicated to the daily existence of the common people. He is a recipient of the 2017 Green Author Prize.

www.ingramcontent.com/pod-product-compliance
Lightning Source LLC
Chambersburg PA
CBHW051350040426
42453CB00007B/500